ANIMAL HUNTERS

Written by Jenny Wood

Illustrated by
Mike Atkinson, Jim Channell
and Robert Cook

HAMLYN

Published in 1992 by
Hamlyn Children's Books,
part of Reed International Books,
Michelin House, 81 Fulham Road,
London SW3 6RB

Produced for Hamlyn Children's Books by Oyster Books

Consultant: Dr Julian Hector

Design: Designworks!, Cheltenham

ISBN 0 600 57390 7

Paper Back ISBN 0 600 57687 6

Printed in Belgium

Contents

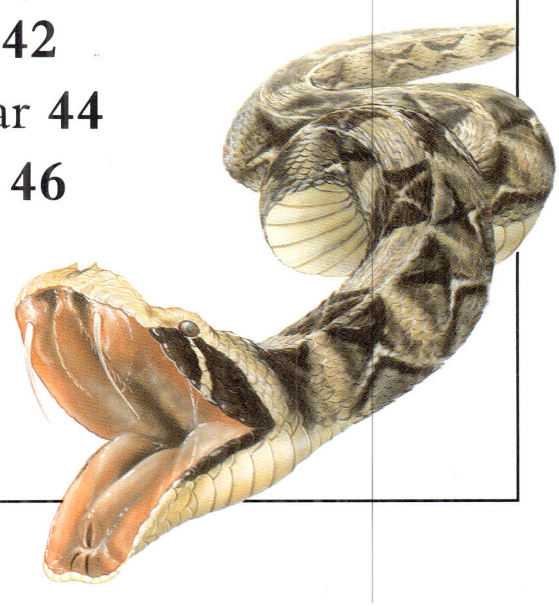

Introduction

Animals are divided into two main groups — those which eat plants, and those which eat meat. The meat-eaters, or carnivores, as they are often called, are the hunters. This book looks at some of the most skilful hunters in the animal kingdom.

Animal hunters come in all shapes and sizes, and are found in every kind of habitat. Their bodies are designed to suit the environment in which they live and the hunting life they lead. They are alert creatures and, in their own different ways, stronger and faster than the animals they hunt. They have to be, because failure to kill means failure to eat, and that can mean death to the hunter.

Animal hunters track down and capture their prey with the help of highly tuned senses and a fascinating range of skills. Some have excellent eyesight. Others have such good hearing that they can find prey by following the echoes made by sound waves bouncing off the prey's body. Some have such a strong sense of smell that they can detect the scent of prey over a distance of several kilometres. Others can locate prey by following a heat trail from the prey's body. Some track down prey by feeling the vibrations the prey makes as it moves around.

Animal hunters kill quickly and efficiently. They stab, stun, squeeze, bite, sting, strangle and crush using a fearsome array of weapons such as razor-edged teeth, sharp claws, poison fangs, powerful jaws and deadly stings.

Most animal hunters lead solitary lives, hunting alone and meeting other members of their own species only to mate. Some live in small family groups, sharing their kill amongst themselves. A few animal hunters live in large groups. This allows them to hunt prey much larger than themselves.

Some of the passages in this book may seem violent. You may begin to think that hunting animals are cruel creatures. But hunting and killing for food is a necessary part of an animal hunter's life. Hunting animals take only what they need to keep themselves and their young alive. The only animals which kill for pleasure, and hunt other animals for fun, are the most dangerous hunters of all — humans.

The Scorpion

As the sun sinks below the horizon, the scorching heat of the desert day fades rapidly and the burning sands begin to cool. Insects, spiders and other small creatures which have avoided the daytime heat by sheltering under rocks and plants or in burrows emerge from their hiding places to begin their nightly search for food.

Suddenly, a fearsome hunter appears out of the gloom and darts into their midst, its poison-tipped tail arched high above its back. The hunter scuttles forward, seizing a fat spider with its powerful pincers. The deadly tail stabs fiercely downwards, the sharp tip piercing the spider's flesh and injecting venom into the struggling body. The spider's struggles grow feeble as the paralysing poison takes effect. The scorpion pulls the body of its prey towards its clicking mouthparts and begins to feed.

There are over 1,000 species of

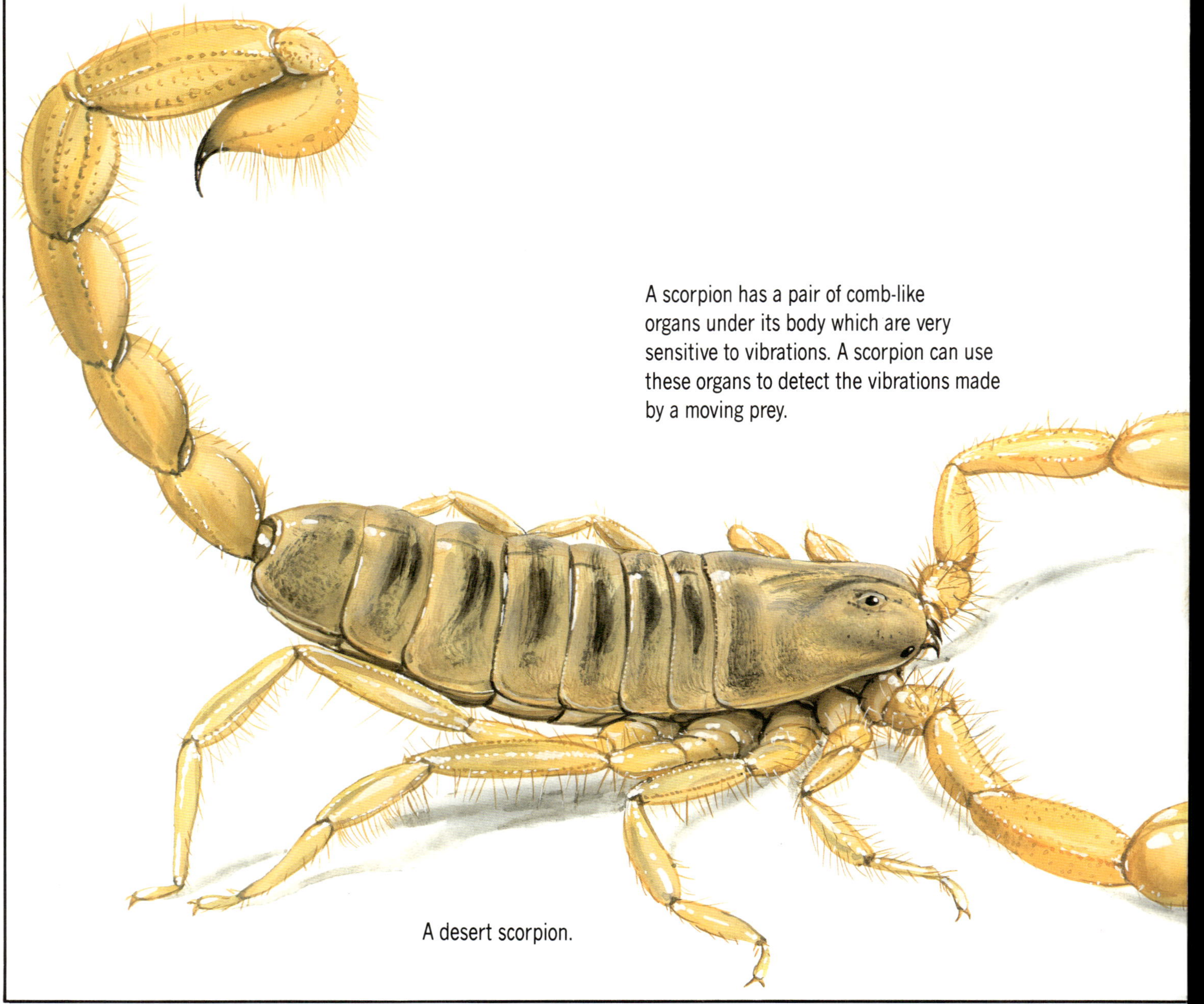

A scorpion has a pair of comb-like organs under its body which are very sensitive to vibrations. A scorpion can use these organs to detect the vibrations made by a moving prey.

A desert scorpion.

scorpion which live mainly in hot, desert areas of the world. Scorpions, which are related to spiders, have four pairs of legs and a pair of powerful, grasping pincers. A scorpion's body is protected by a covering of tough, horny armour. All scorpions have a poisonous sting which they carry in their tail. Most species of scorpion have only a mild venom, but the Durango scorpion of Mexico and the Austral scorpion of North Africa have stings which can kill a human.

A scorpion's sting is found on the curved, pointed end of the creature's tail. Two glands at the base of the sting produce poison. These glands carry the poison to an opening near the tip of the sting. As the scorpion's sting pierces the flesh of the prey, the poison flows out of the sting and into the prey's body.

A scorpion eats by tearing at a prey with its mouthparts, injecting digestive juices into the body of the victim, then sucking the body dry.

The top of the front part of a scorpion's body is formed by a shield that carries one pair of eyes in the middle and between three to five pairs along the sides. In some scorpions, some of the side eyes are barely visible.

The Bird-Eating Spider

The bird sits on her nest, incubating her eggs. She is unaware of the deadly hunter creeping slowly and silently along the branch towards her. She senses a sudden movement, but too late! The giant spider pounces. Its fangs stab down, injecting a deadly poison into its victim's body. Within a few minutes the bird lies still. Then the spider's mouthparts, acting as straws, suck the fluids from the bird's dead body until only feathers and bone are left.

Bird-eating spiders are found only in hot countries. Most are forest-dwellers, though some live in desert areas. The largest specimens lurk in the rainforests of South America. Bird-eating spiders normally hunt by night, preying on birds, small reptiles, beetles, moths, grasshoppers and other spiders. They have hairy bodies and, when attacked, can shed their hairs. These hairs contain chemicals which irritate the eyes, noses and skin of other creatures. Bird-eating spiders are quite short-sighted, so their eyes are useful only when they are close to their prey, ready to make the final killing pounce. Although they have no noses or ears, spiders can 'smell' through organs in their legs. They also use the hairs on their bodies to detect vibrations made by the movements of their prey.

When a bird-eating spider attacks, it raises the front half of its body and holds its front legs high in the air. It then plunges its poison fangs downwards into the body of its prey.

An opening in the tip of each fang connects with poison glands in the spider's body. When the spider stabs a prey, poison flows down the fangs and into the wound. The victim is soon paralysed.

Bird-eating spiders are the largest of all spiders. They are hairy, thick-legged creatures which can grow as big as an adult human hand.

The Ant Lion

The hunter scuttles backwards over the rocky ground until it reaches a patch of sandy soil. Then, still walking backwards, it moves round and round in circles, digging out a funnel-shaped pit with its pointed tail. When the pit is finished, the hunter digs a hole in the sandy bottom. It lies there, waiting in ambush. Soon a wandering ant approaches. The pit's soft, sandy sides give way under the ant's weight and the ant is sucked inside. Instantly, the hunter springs out from its hiding place and, with its long, sharp jaws, bites off the ant's head.

The ant lion is the larva of the ant lion fly, a flying insect which looks rather like a dragonfly. Ant lion flies and their larvae are found in most of the world's warm countries, but especially in tropical areas. The ant lion larva has a plump, hairy body. It is a ferocious hunter which feeds on ants and other small insects. Its head is long and narrow, and armed with long, sword-like jaws. Its six legs are positioned close behind its head, three on each side. One of the most unusual things about the ant lion larva is that it only moves backwards!

1 As it moves backwards, the ant lion uses its pointed tail to dig into the sand.

2 The sand slides up and over the creature's hairy back. Every few seconds the ant lion flicks its head, to fling the sand away to the side.

3 As the ant lion digs, it moves in smaller and smaller circles to form the funnel shape of its trap.

4 The finished trap.

When the ant lion lies in wait at the bottom of its pit, only its long jaws can be seen sticking out of the sand. Its mouthparts contain tubes which suck the juices from its prey.

The White Piranha

As dawn breaks, the capybara trots down to the river's edge and wades into the water in search of food. But its movements have been detected by a band of fearsome hunters lurking below the surface. Two of the hunters, hungrier and bolder than their companions, move swiftly towards the unsuspecting creature. As their razor-sharp teeth slice into its legs, the capybara starts with terror and tries to swim back to the bank. But there is no escape. Drawn by the scent of blood in the water, the rest of the hunters race to join the attack. The hungry shoal of white piranhas surround the capybara and begin to feed.

White piranhas live in the murky waters of the River Amazon in South America. They grow up to a length of about 60 centimetres. They are ferocious hunters, who always seem to be hungry. There is some evidence to suggest that these fish never stop growing, which may explain their huge appetites. Piranhas normally feed on other fish, but they will also attack large animals, such as capybaras, who enter the river water. Capybaras, the world's largest rodents, are powerful swimmers. But even they are no match for a large shoal of piranhas in a 'feeding frenzy' which can strip the flesh from a large animal in only a few minutes.

White piranhas are the feared killers of the Amazon. Their powerful jaws are armed with small, triangular, needle-sharp teeth.

A piranha homes in on its prey with amazing speed, helped by its good eyesight and strong sense of smell. A piranha is also able to feel vibrations caused by other creatures moving through the water.

A shoal of piranhas may have between 500 and 1,000 members. Piranhas seem to be able to recognize members of their own shoal, and will attack 'strange' piranhas from other groups.

The American Alligator

The muddy waters of the river seem empty, apart from a few rotting logs floating by the bank. The pig trots down to the water and wades in to take a long, cooling drink. Very slowly, one of the logs drifts away from the bank. All of a sudden, the peaceful scene is shattered. There is an explosion of activity as the 'log' comes to life in a burst of spray. Giant jaws armed with fearsome teeth seize the pig's leg and drag the squealing animal into the murky depths. The water churns as the American alligator rolls its prey over and over, tearing off the limb which will be its meal.

American alligators live in the rivers and swamps of Florida and other coastal regions of the southern USA. They eat many kinds of small animal that live in and near water including fish, snakes, frogs, turtles, small mammals and birds. Sometimes large male alligators will also attack dogs, pigs or even cattle which stray into the water.

Male alligators are enormous creatures. They may be as long as 3.7 metres and weigh up to 250 kilos. They live for about 60 years.

Alligators are able to live on land as well as in water, but most of their hunting is done in water, where they can lurk unseen. An alligator drags its victim under the surface and holds it there until it drowns. It then tears the creature to pieces.

The eyes of an alligator stick up above its skull. This allows the creature to lie in ambush in the water and watch its prey approaching.

Alligators have broad, strong jaws which are useful for seizing and holding large prey. They have about 100 teeth but these are not the right shape for cutting flesh or for chewing, so an alligator twists chunks of meat from the body of its prey and swallows the chunks whole. Alligators often lose teeth when hunting, but they have small, new teeth growing under the old ones, and these quickly fill the gaps.

The Archer Fish

Insects buzz and flit unsuspectingly through the branches which overhang the calm surface of the murky pool. But underwater, invisible to the insects above, a hunter swims slowly along. It rises smoothly to the surface and looks around. Its keen eyes soon spot a small dragonfly resting on a leaf. The hunter moves into position and, with its whip-like tongue, fires a stream of water droplets at the insect. The dragonfly, stunned by one of the droplets, falls to the surface. The hungry archer fish swims towards the floating body and gobbles it down.

The archer fish, found mainly in India, Malaysia and Australia, has an unusual method of catching its prey. The fish stuns the insects it eats by shooting drops of water from its mouth. These watery bullets travel with great force and can even stun an insect while it is moving through the air. Archer fish are found in both salt and fresh water. They have excellent eyesight and can see as well underwater as they can above the surface. They often eat water creatures, such as worms and shrimps, but prefer resting or flying insects.

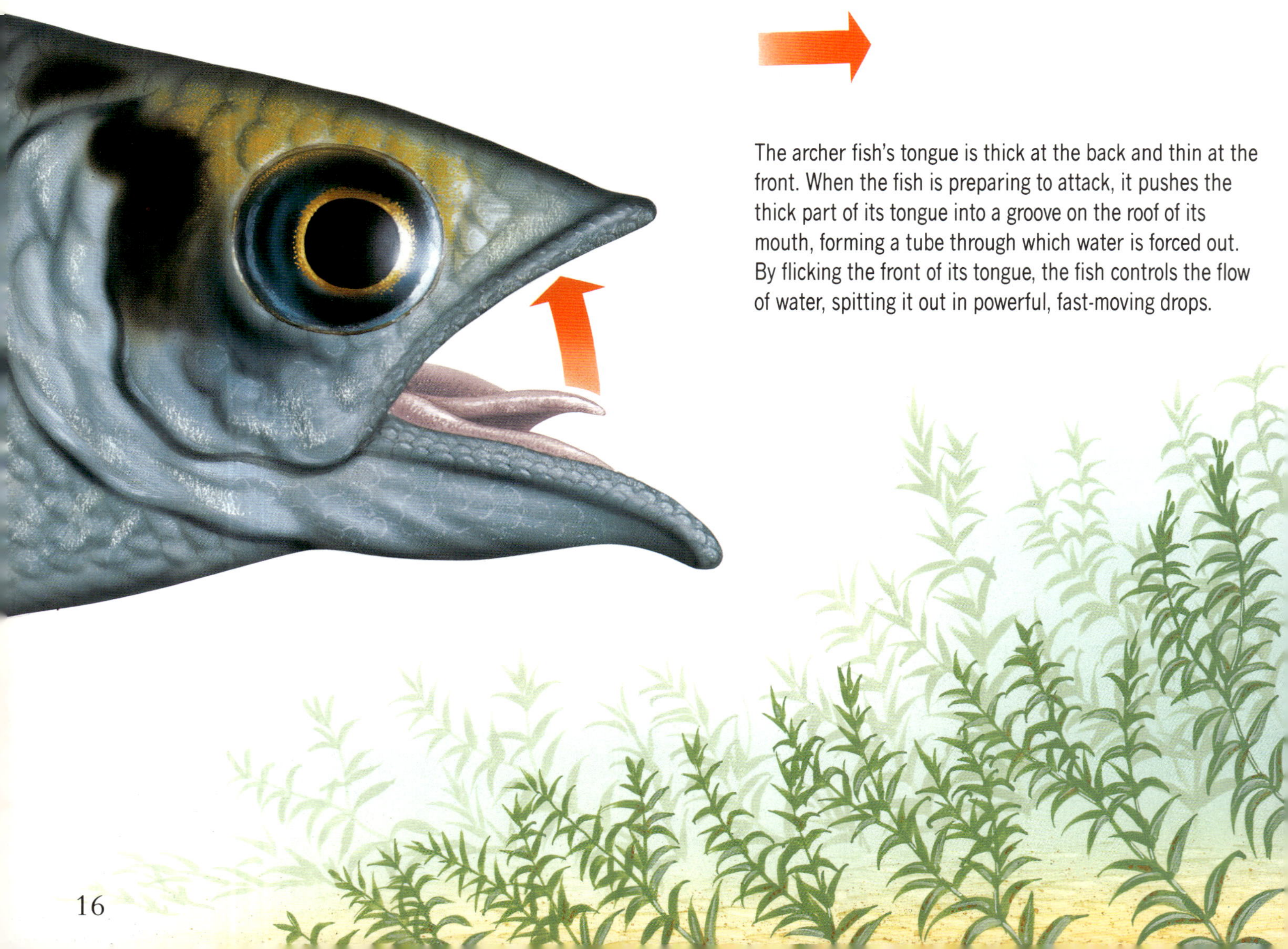

The archer fish's tongue is thick at the back and thin at the front. When the fish is preparing to attack, it pushes the thick part of its tongue into a groove on the roof of its mouth, forming a tube through which water is forced out. By flicking the front of its tongue, the fish controls the flow of water, spitting it out in powerful, fast-moving drops.

An archer fish prepares to shoot at an insect by swimming until it is in a position just below the victim. Keeping its large eyes fixed firmly on the insect, the fish tilts its body into an almost vertical position and rises until the tip of its snout touches the surface of the water. With its head pointing towards the insect, the fish takes aim. An adult archer fish can shoot down an insect from as far away as 1.5 metres, but young archer fish can only 'shoot' accurately over a distance of a few centimetres.

Sometimes, rather than shooting down an insect, an archer fish will jump out of the water and snatch the insect with its jaws.

The Meerkat

The sentries stand alert on the patch of high ground, keeping watch in case a bird of prey should swoop down without warning from the blazing sky and try to attack the group's young. Nearby, other members of the group forage for food in the dry, sun-baked soil. One of the slim hunters corners a scorpion. It dances round the deadly creature, making short rushes to attack, then skipping back quickly out of range of the scorpion's stabbing sting. Finally the hunter darts in and, with one bite, neatly removes the scorpion's tail. The meerkat seizes the now defenceless scorpion and begins to eat.

Meerkats, which are a type of mongoose, are found in southern Africa. They live in large family groups, in shallow, underground burrows which they dig with their strong, curved claws. Meerkats are fierce hunters. They mainly eat spiders and insects, but will also catch small mammals and reptiles. They may even attack animals much larger than themselves, such as wild cats and wild dogs, if those animals threaten the family group. Unlike most hunting animals, meerkats give no warning or special display to show they are going to attack.

When attacking a scorpion, a meerkat manoeuvres itself into a position where it is able to bite off the scorpion's tail without being stung. Once its sting is removed, the scorpion is no longer fully able to defend itself.

Meerkats live in well-organized groups. Each member of the group has a job to do. Some act as sentries, some hunt, and others look after the young.

Meerkats hunt in the morning and in the evening, when the sun's heat is less fierce. They usually work in teams to corner and kill their prey.

The Bengal Tiger

The tall grasses part as the hunter passes silently through, his sensitive nostrils alert to the scent of prey carried by the gentle breeze. As he approaches the nearby river, he sees the herd of sambar by the water's edge. At once he crouches amongst the reeds, absolutely still. An hour goes by. At last the tiger tenses his powerful muscles, twitches his tail and pulls back on his haunches. In a blur of speed, he leaps out from his cover, claws extended. The sambar flee, but for one of them it is too late. Powerful front paws hurtle into the creature's side, stunning it and knocking it to the ground. Fearsome jaws then close around its neck. With one bite, the struggle is over.

The tiger is the largest member of the cat family, and is one of the most skilled hunters in the animal kingdom. There are not many wild tigers left in the world today, but all are found in Asia. The Bengal tiger, which lives in the hot, grassy jungles of India, is the most numerous. Tigers prefer to hunt large prey such as antelope, deer, wild oxen and wild pig, but they will also kill smaller creatures such as monkeys and frogs if food is scarce. Tigers usually hunt at night and rest during the day. They pull the dead bodies of their prey under cover before eating, so they can eat without being disturbed. Unlike lions, which live in groups, tigers prefer to live and hunt alone.

The sambar is a type of deer. Although sambars are alert creatures and can run fast, they are not always able to escape from a surprise attack by a powerful Bengal tiger.

A tiger has very good eyesight, and can see ahead as well as to the side. This helps the tiger judge distances accurately when pouncing on its prey.

A tiger's claws are normally pulled back inside folds of skin between its toes. But when the tiger attacks, the claws are pushed forwards, to help the animal grip its prey.

During the day, a tiger can see about as well as a human being. But at night, its sight is six times better than ours. Its pupils open wide, to let in as much light as possible.

A tiger has two large front teeth, known as fang teeth. These are perfectly positioned so that the distance between them is exactly the same as the distance between the neck joints of the tiger's usual prey. One bite means instant death, as the animal's neck is broken.

The Great Diving Beetle

The great diving beetle is one of the largest and fiercest of all underwater insects. It is found only in clean, unpolluted water.

The armoured hunter whirrs through the air, in search of a new pond in which to feed. The search does not take long. The hunter banks towards the water below. It splashes on to the surface then dives, its rounded, streamlined body propelled through the water by thrusts of its rear legs. The hunter is hungry after its journey. Its eyes scan the depths, while its antennae 'taste' the water for traces of a possible prey. Catching the scent trail of a small fish, the hunter races through the water, until the fish is in sight. Reaching out with its strong front legs, the hunter grasps the fish and pulls the squirming creature towards its powerful jaws. The great diving beetle begins to munch the still live prey.

The great diving beetle is found in open water in ponds, ditches and rivers throughout Europe. It is a fierce hunter, not only in its adult form, but also in its larval stage, and is often known as the 'tiger' of the underwater world. It preys on fish, frogs, newts and the larvae of other insects, often catching and killing creatures much larger than itself. The great diving beetle breathes air and must return to the surface regularly. It stores a bubble of air under its wings, and can stay underwater for up to 45 minutes at a time. Its only real enemies are wading birds and ducks.

The great diving beetle uses the stiff hairs on its back legs like oars, to paddle through the water.

The larva of the great diving beetle is also a fierce hunter. It may grow as long as five centimetres, and is able to overpower creatures the same size as, or even larger than, itself. Its jaws are pointed, hollow tubes, through which it sucks the body contents of its prey into its mouth. Great diving beetle larvae are found on the beds of ponds and streams.

The Killer Whale

Driven by powerful thrusts of its huge tail, the hunter cruises through the dark, icy waters of the Arctic sea. Its eyes cannot see far through the gloom, but its ears are alert for the sound of likely prey. Suddenly, the hunter accelerates, surging through the water. By following the trail of sound made by a fleeing seal, the hunter is soon able to home in on its target. The seal, sensing danger, heads for the surface and the safety of an ice floe. But too late! The hunter seizes the seal in its wickedly pointed teeth. With one gulp, the seal is eaten. The killer whale scans the ocean ahead for new prey.

Killer whales are the largest members of the dolphin family, and may grow up to nine metres in length. They are found in all the world's oceans, but seem to prefer the cold seas around the Arctic and Antarctic. A thick layer of fat, called blubber, which lies under their skin, keeps them warm in the icy water. Killer whales often travel in groups called pods, each of which may contain over 100 whales. They usually hunt in groups, too, feeding mainly on salmon, dolphins, seals, walruses and sea birds. Killer whales are ferocious hunters. As well as attacking in open water, they may ride on the waves to the edge of a beach and carry off young seals. Killer whales have no sense of smell and only poor eyesight. They hunt mainly by using a system of sounds and echoes known as echo-location.

Killer whales belong to a group known as toothed whales. A killer whale has between 40 and 50 large, cone-shaped teeth in its mouth, which it uses to capture slippery prey. Killer whales do not chew their food. Instead, they swallow it whole.

A killer whale tracks down its prey mainly by sound. The whale makes a series of high-pitched sounds which travel forwards through the water. When the beams of sound reach an object, an echo bounces back from the object to the whale. The echo is picked up by sensitive points on the whale's chin and under its fins, and carried to the whale's inner ears. The echo tells the whale in which direction it must travel to reach the object, and how far away the object is.

The Emerald Tree Boa

The rainforest is alive with movement. Monkeys swing through the trees. Birds perch in the leafy canopy, calling to each other. One brightly-coloured bird flits from branch to branch, catching insects, unaware of the danger lurking ahead. Coiled around a branch, a deadly hunter waits for its next meal. The green and white markings on its body are a perfect disguise against the forest leaves. The bird swoops within reach. The hunter's head shoots out, mouth gaping wide. Sharp teeth pierce the feathery skin. The hunter then coils itself around its victim and squeezes tight. The bird struggles briefly then, unable to breathe, becomes still. The emerald tree boa swallows its meal.

The emerald tree boa is found in the rainforests of South America. It is a skilful climber and spends most of its life in the trees. It is one of a group of snakes known as constrictors, most of which are large and powerful. A constrictor kills by coiling its body round its prey and squeezing until the victim suffocates. When the emerald tree boa hunts, it grips a branch with its strong tail, coils part of its body around the branch then suspends the rest of its body in mid-air. As a prey passes, the snake shoots its head forward and attacks. Most types of tree boa hunt mainly at night. During the heat of the day, they rest amongst the shady leaves, coiled around a branch.

A constrictor, such as the emerald tree boa, has a huge number of bones and muscles in its body. These make it possible for the snake to bend and twist in many different directions.

A snake's prey often looks too big to fit into its mouth. But, before eating, a snake detaches its upper jaw from its lower jaw. It can then stretch its mouth open very wide indeed. When it has finished eating, the snake yawns to bring its jaws back into position.

The emerald tree boa eats birds and small mammals. It is the fastest moving of all boas, and is also a strong swimmer.

The Assassin Bug

As the bee flits from flower to flower, searching for nectar, its antennae pick up an irresistible scent. The bee banks and flies towards the source, skimming along the scent trail until it reaches the flower. It lands, unaware of the deadly assassin waiting in ambush inside the flower head. Suddenly, strong forelimbs seize the bee, and a long, curved beak stabs deep into its abdomen. The assassin bug begins to suck the juices from the struggling body of its prey.

There are over 4,000 species of assassin bug. These brightly-coloured hunters live mainly in tropical regions. Most assassin bugs are active hunters which attack slow-moving prey, such as caterpillars. Some, such as the bee-killer assassin bug, hide in flowers and ambush their prey. Many species of assassin bug can give off powerful scents. Some produce unpleasant smells which scare away predators. Others, such as the bee-killer, give off scents to attract prey.

This 'hissing' assassin bug can make a hissing noise by rubbing its rostrum against rough parts of its body.

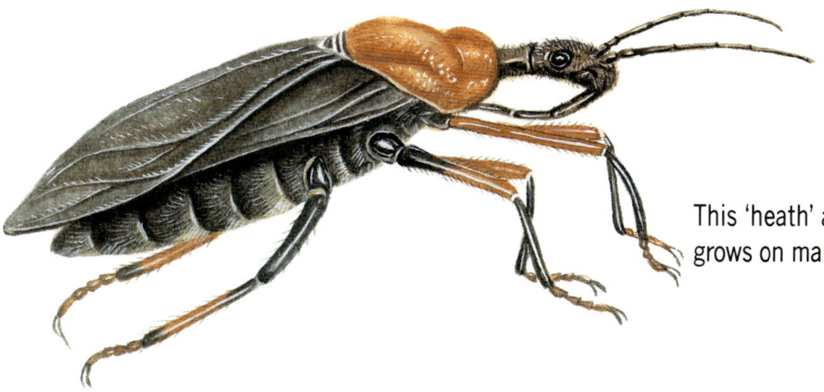

This 'heath' assassin bug lives amongst the heather which grows on many hills and moorland areas in Britain.

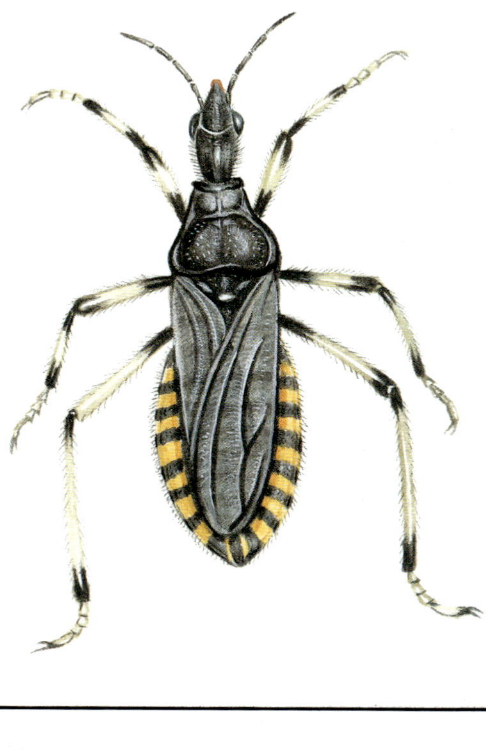

A slender-legged assassin bug.

Many species of assassin bug have stout bodies and can attack quite large millipedes or caterpillars. Others have long, slender legs which they may use to pick food from spiders' webs.

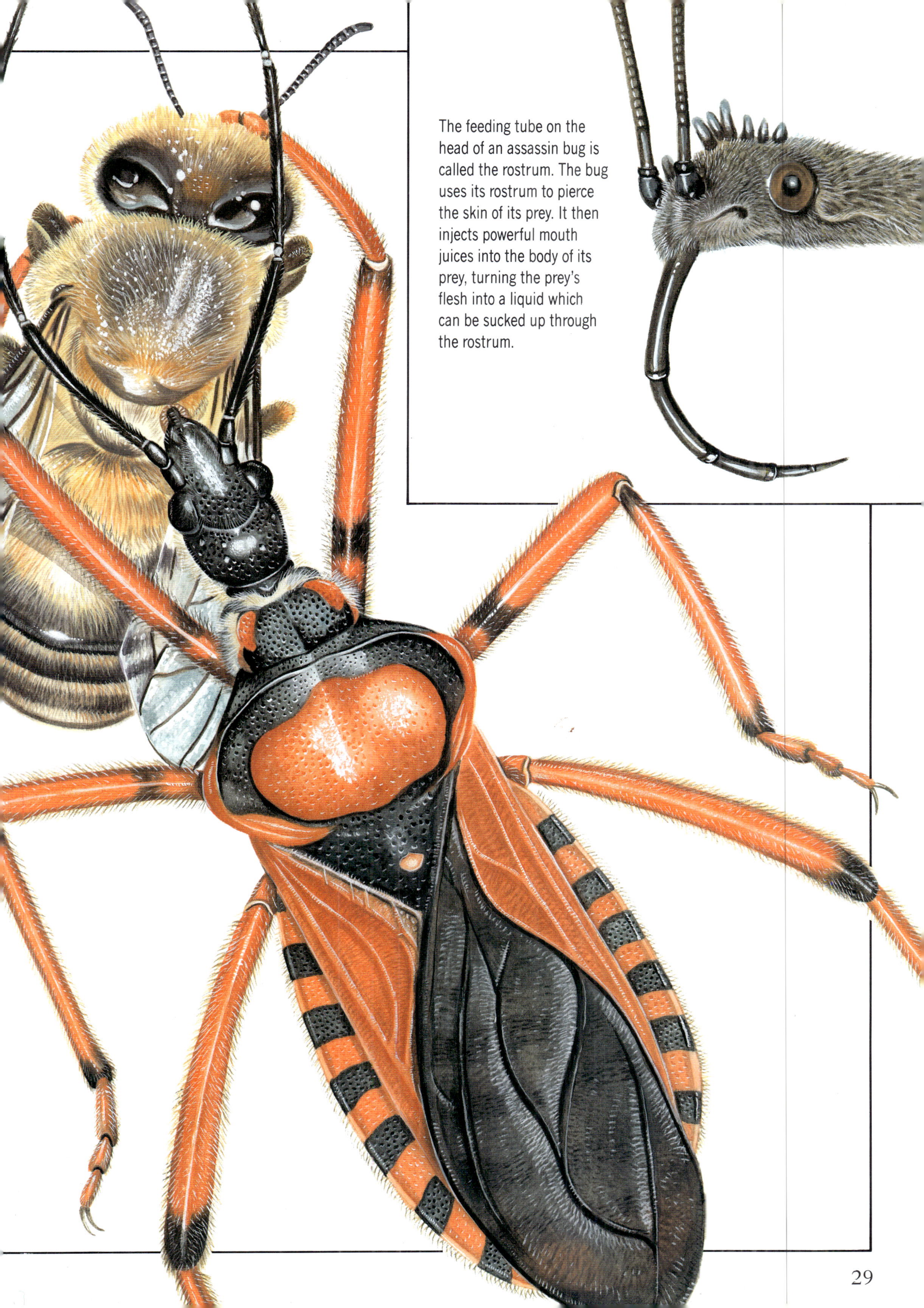

The feeding tube on the head of an assassin bug is called the rostrum. The bug uses its rostrum to pierce the skin of its prey. It then injects powerful mouth juices into the body of its prey, turning the prey's flesh into a liquid which can be sucked up through the rostrum.

The Atlantic Octopus

The soft body of the hunter, propelled by its delicately waving arms, seems to tiptoe across the sea bed. The creature reaches a deep cleft in the rock and slides inside. Gradually its skin changes colour until it matches perfectly the rocks amongst which it lies, watching and waiting. Its keen eyes soon spot a crab moving slowly past. The hunter shoots out from its hiding place like an underwater jet, its muscular arms reaching out and wrapping themselves around the prey. The crab struggles feebly but the suckers on the hunter's arms hold it in a vice-like grip. There is no escape. The powerful arms of the Atlantic octopus break the crab's shell, tearing it apart so the sharp beak can reach the tender, living flesh below.

There are about 50 species of octopus, all of which live in salt water. They are usually found near the sea bed, lying in wait for slow-moving prey. The body of an octopus has no bones. Instead, it is covered with a tough, protective skin called the mantle. The mantle contains many tiny bags of colouring called pigment which allow an octopus to change colour when hiding from prey or escaping from a predator. An octopus has eight arms, each of which is lined with suckers. These suckers grip the shellfish, crabs and lobsters which the octopus eats.

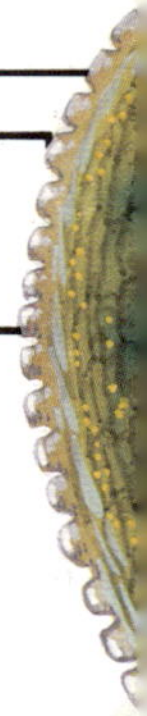

An octopus swims backwards! It moves by drawing water into its body then squeezing the water out through an opening called the siphon, which lies under its head. The force with which the water leaves the octopus's body pushes the creature backwards.

The suckers on the undersides of an octopus's arms are rows of round muscles. An octopus uses its suckers for gripping tightly on to its prey.

An octopus's mouth is hidden on the underside of its body. At the opening to the mouth is a sharp, horny beak with which the octopus bites into the flesh of its prey. Some species of octopus spit poison into their prey, as they bite.

An octopus can squeeze its soft body into very small spaces which are perfect for ambush.

As well as having good eyesight, an octopus has special sense organs called 'pits', one below each eye. As the octopus moves, water passes in and out of these organs. The organs 'taste' the water and detect traces of likely prey.

The Spotted Hyena

The hunter moves cautiously along the fringe of the huge herd of zebra and wildebeest. The grazing animals stir nervously as they catch a strange scent on the wind. The zebra bunch together, but the wildebeest scatter in panic. One old wildebeest runs more slowly than the rest. The hunter begins to chase, snapping at the wildebeest's heels with sharp teeth. Other members of the hunter's clan join in the chase, darting forward and wounding the wildebeest by biting savagely at its hindquarters. Exhausted and bleeding, the wildebeest sinks to the ground. The pack of spotted hyenas swarm over their prey, ripping open the animal's stomach with their powerful teeth, and tearing off chunks of flesh. Within ten minutes, the wildebeest is reduced to a skeleton.

Spotted hyenas are found in Africa, in the countries south of the Sahara Desert. They live in large packs of up to 50 animals, led by the most powerful female member of the group. At one time it was thought that hyenas were scavengers which only ate the remains of animals killed by other hunters such as lions. We now know that hyenas are skilful hunters in their own right. They eat almost anything, from insects to water buffalo. Hyenas are strong runners. In order to catch large, powerful animals, hyenas hunt as a group, taking it in turns to wound the fleeing prey until the animal becomes exhausted. When hunting zebra, which tend to bunch together into defensive groups, hyenas attack in much larger numbers to make sure of the kill.

Spotted hyenas are noisy animals. They communicate with each other by howling when preparing to attack, and by making eerie 'laughing' sounds as they kill.

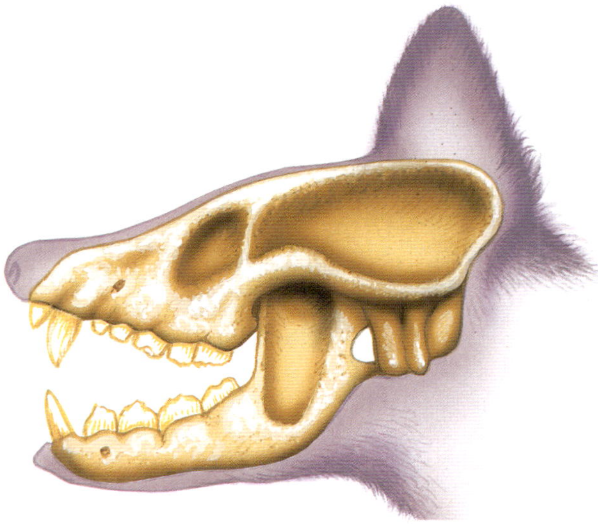

A spotted hyena has very large cheek teeth. These allow the animal to crush bone and tear through tough hide.

A spotted hyena has strong neck and shoulder muscles, to help it pull to the ground a prey much larger than itself.

The Great White Shark

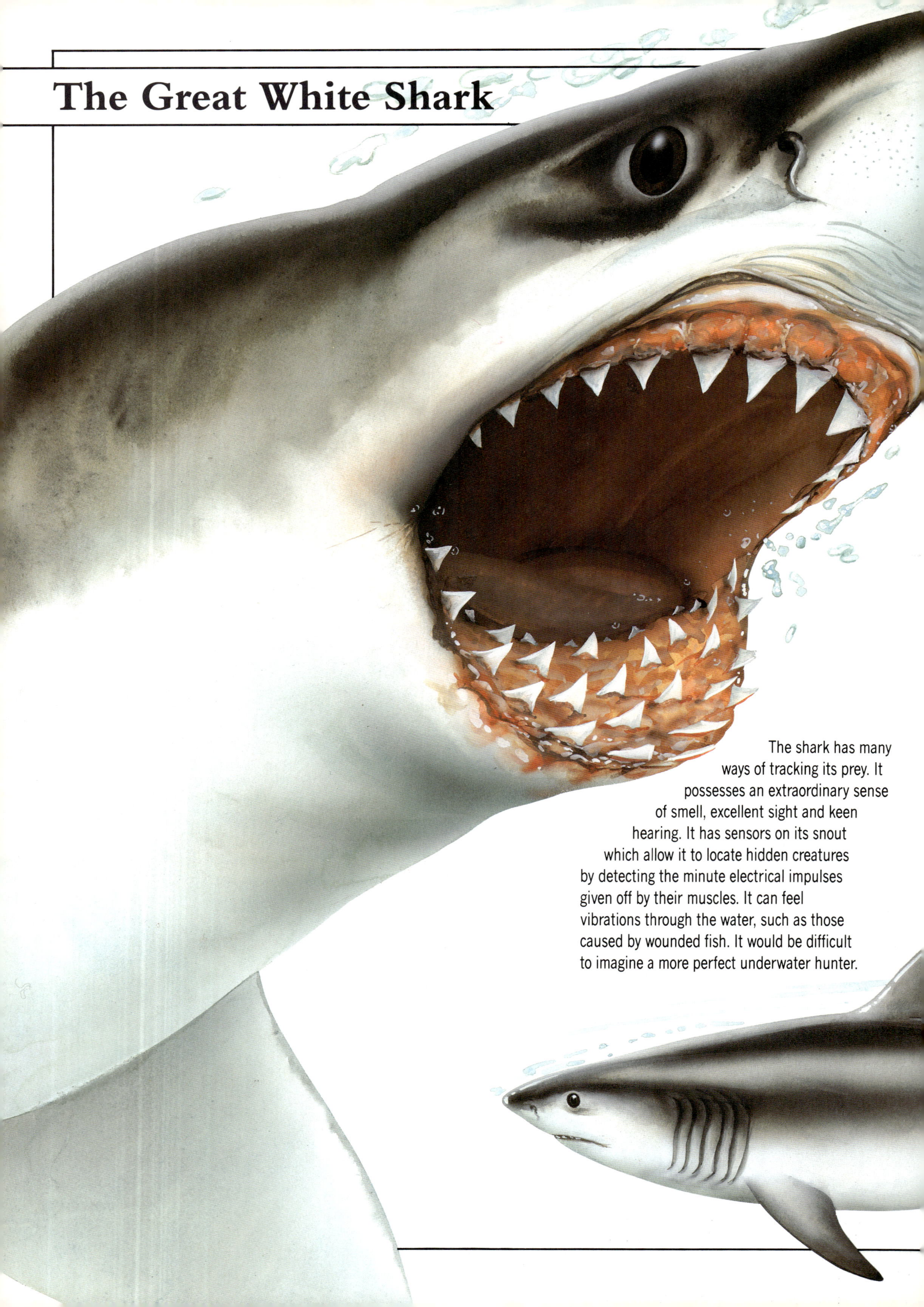

The shark has many ways of tracking its prey. It possesses an extraordinary sense of smell, excellent sight and keen hearing. It has sensors on its snout which allow it to locate hidden creatures by detecting the minute electrical impulses given off by their muscles. It can feel vibrations through the water, such as those caused by wounded fish. It would be difficult to imagine a more perfect underwater hunter.

Three metres below the surface of the ocean a long, streamlined shape glides through the water. Its powerful tail moves steadily from side to side, propelling the sleek body along. The hunter is alert for the tiniest movement, the faintest scent of distant prey.

Suddenly the giant fish accelerates through the water. Its amazing senses have detected a source of food. Ahead, a seal swims desperately, but it has no hope of escaping from the perfect underwater killing machine which surges towards it. The great white shark opens its gigantic jaws and strikes.

There are 344 known species of shark. They vary in size from the giant whale shark, which can grow to over 18 metres in length, to the spined pigmy shark which never grows longer than 25 centimetres. Sharks are found in all the world's oceans. Some hunt in shallow water, others in the ocean depths. Most sharks feed on fish as well as turtles and seabirds, but large sharks, such as the great white, will eat seals, sea lions and other sharks. Although widely feared, sharks seldom attack humans. The three most dangerous species are the great white, the tiger shark and the bull shark which between them make about 30 attacks each year.

All sharks have at least five sets of teeth in their jaws at any one time. When a shark loses a tooth, a replacement moves forward to take its place. Every shark produces hundreds of sets of teeth in its lifetime. The size and shape of a shark's teeth depends on the food it eats. The great white captures its prey by sinking its dagger-shaped teeth into the creature's skin. It then shakes its head violently and, as it does so, the serrated edges of its teeth saw through sections of flesh.

As the great white swims, the ocean currents carry the smell of a prey to its super-sensitive nostrils in the same way that the wind brings a scent to a lion or tiger. When it detects a scent it turns into the current, moving rapidly towards the source of the smell. Sharks can follow an underwater scent over several kilometres.

The Peregrine Falcon

High above the rocky cliff, the peregrine falcon soars on the rising air currents. Its keen eyes scan the sky until it sees a bird flying far below. The falcon folds back its wings and dives towards its prey. As it approaches the flying bird, the falcon spreads out its wings and large, curved talons, braking violently. A hind toe strikes the bird on the spine. There is an explosion of feathers as the peregrine falcon seizes its prey in a grip of iron, and flies back to its nest.

The peregrine falcon is one of the most spectacular killers in the bird kingdom. During its steep attacking dive, called a stoop, it can reach a speed of 200 kilometres per hour. Like all falcons, the peregrine has excellent eyesight and can spot a likely meal at a great distance. Peregrines mostly hunt other birds. They grip their prey with their powerful talons, then use their sharp, hooked beak to tear at the flesh.

The peregrine falcon can look separately out of each eye, and so can see to the left and to the right at the same time. It uses both eyes together when it looks straight ahead.

Like most birds of prey, the peregrine falcon has four toes. Each is armed with a long, curved claw called a talon. The talon on the back toe is used like a dagger to stab the prey. The talons on the three front toes are used for gripping.

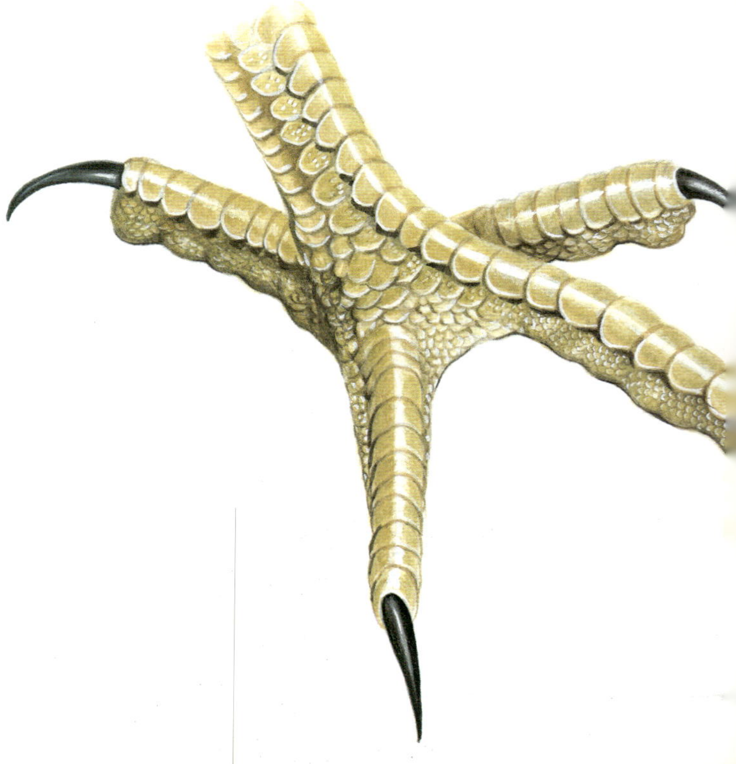

During a stoop, the peregrine falcon narrows its tail and holds its wings close to its body to create a more streamlined shape. This allows the bird to dive through the air at great speed. When it approaches its prey, the falcon slows down by spreading out its wings and talons.

The Army Ant

It is dawn. Already the army of blind ants is on the move. Ahead of the main body of warriors, the scouts seek out a likely prey. They find their way by tapping the ground with their antennae, then lay a scent trail for the soldiers to follow. When the soldiers have advanced about 30 metres, all the ants spread out and begin to hunt. Any insects in their path are attacked, bitten to death, then sliced up for food. Some of the pieces are eaten straightaway, others are carried back to the home base to feed the queen and the soldiers left behind to protect her. The killing continues day after day until the area has been stripped bare of food. Then it is time for the army ants to move on to new hunting grounds.

Army ants are found in Africa and South America. They are fierce hunters who will attack any likely source of food. They can destroy wasps' nests and have even been known to kill animals as large as dogs. Their home base is often made of a living mass of ants, in the centre of which is the queen who spends all her time laying eggs. When the eggs begin to develop into grubs, extra food is needed and so the whole ant community moves through the forest in search of fresh prey. The ants travel for two or three weeks, making a temporary camp every night. When the grubs start to become pupae, the ants rest for a few days. As the pupae hatch into adults, the queen lays more eggs. The ants must forage for food once more.

An ant's head includes two antennae and a pair of jaws called mandibles. The antennae are used for smelling, touching, tasting and hearing. The mandibles move from side to side rather than up and down. Soldier ants use their strong mandibles as weapons and to slice up their food.

The pieces of solid food which an ant puts into its mouth pass into a small pouch. The muscles in the pouch squeeze out the liquid, which the ant then swallows. The ant spits out the pellet of solid food that is left.

Army ants usually travel in narrow columns, preying on other insects and spiders. They will also kill other, larger animals such as caterpillars which cannot escape quickly. A column of army ants may number as many as 750,000!

The Emperor Dragonfly

The sun flashes off the insect's shining blue body as it swoops across the water. It stops and hovers, looking for food, its magnificent, jewel-like eyes scanning the air for the slightest movement made by likely prey. Suddenly, the insect darts forward at incredible speed, its spiny legs forming a basket beneath its body. A butterfly banks desperately, trying to escape. But it stands no chance against the Emperor dragonfly, one of the fastest and most skilful of all flying insects. Powerful, serrated jaws close around the butterfly's body. The hunter eats.

There are about 2,700 species of dragonfly in the world. Most live in warm countries, near water, where they prey on insects and small water animals. Dragonflies are expert hunters. They have excellent eyesight, and can look in all directions, even backwards. Each eye has over 1,000 lenses! They are expert flyers, too, and can reach speeds of up to 97 kilometres per hour. They can hover, fly backwards and even perform spectacular aerobatics. Dragonflies live in the air, seldom landing, and can eat and even mate while flying at full speed.

A young dragonfly hatches under water, and remains there for up to five years. It has no wings, but it catches prey by shooting out a folding lower lip called a mask, which is half as long as its body. At the end of the mask are vicious hooks which spear the victim.

Dragonflies are unlike other insects in that their wings contain flight muscles similar to those found in the wings of birds. These flight muscles allow the dragonfly to fly quietly and powerfully.

Adult dragonflies are amongst the most beautifully coloured of all insects. They live for only a few months at most.

The Gaboon Viper

The mouse scuttles quickly across the forest floor, unaware of the invisible killer lying in wait among the dead leaves. Suddenly the mouth of the gaboon viper opens, and long fangs swing down from its upper jaw. With terrifying speed, the snake strikes. Its fangs pierce fur and skin, injecting deadly venom into the mouse's body. Then the snake's jaws open, releasing the mouse, which staggers away, already affected by the poison which is now pumping round its body. The viper, its tongue flickering, slithers almost lazily along the scent trail left by its dying prey. Soon the snake will eat again.

There are about 170 species of viper, all of them poisonous. They are found in almost every country in the world, except for Australia. A viper's venom, the mixture of poisons that snakes use to kill their prey, is produced by two glands that lie in the snake's mouth, one on either side of the upper jaw. The venom flows into the hollow fangs, which then squirt the poison into the victim's body. Vipers do not have especially good eyesight or hearing, but rely mainly on their sense of smell to provide them with information about the whereabouts of possible prey.

Gaboon vipers, which live in Africa, have the longest fangs of any snake. The venom which these vipers inject into their victims' bodies affects the victims' ability to breathe. It also damages the victims' blood vessels, causing internal bleeding. Gaboon vipers hunt during the day, relying on their excellent camouflage to confuse their prey.

People often think that a snake's skin is wet and slimy. In fact, a snake's skin is dry and is made up of hundreds of tiny, overlapping scales.

Like all snakes, vipers have a keen sense of smell. They can smell through their nostrils but they also stick out their tongues to pick up scents in the air or on the ground. When a viper pulls its tongue back in, the traces of scent are picked up by two hollow sacs in the roof of its mouth. These sacs are known as the Jacobson's organ. This organ helps the snake to follow the scent of its prey.

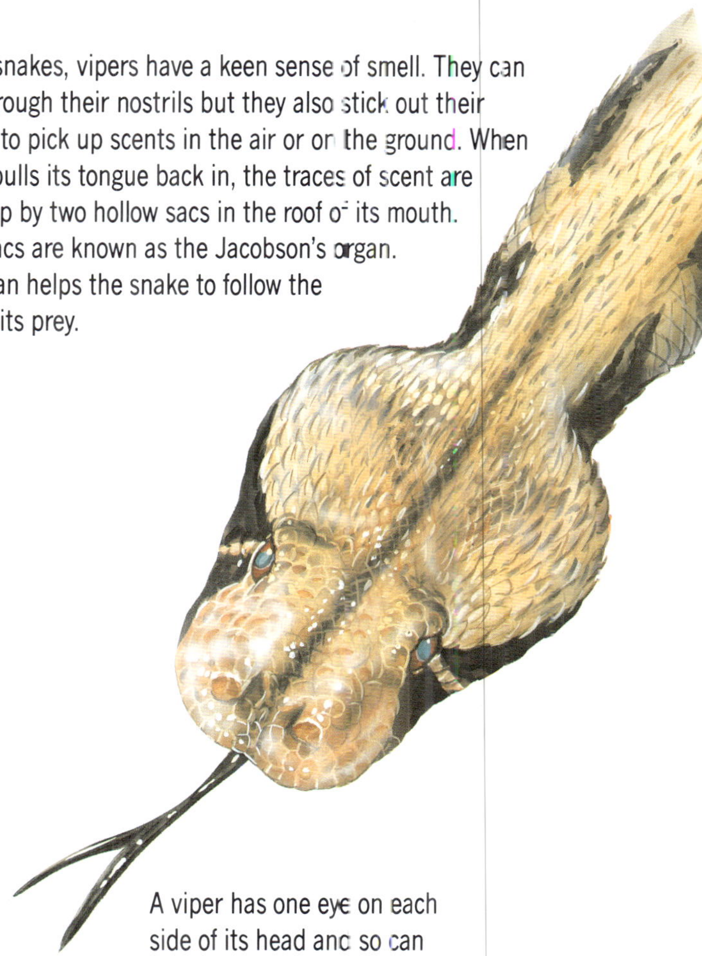

A viper has one eye on each side of its head and so can see in almost every direction. But although they can easily see movement, vipers cannot focus their eyes on individual objects very well.

A viper's long, hollow front fangs fold back against the roof of its mouth when not in use. The fangs swing forward when the snake strikes.

The Common Sea Star

A sea star's arms are often damaged or broken while looking for food or escaping from a predator. But sea stars are able to grow new arms to replace the old ones!

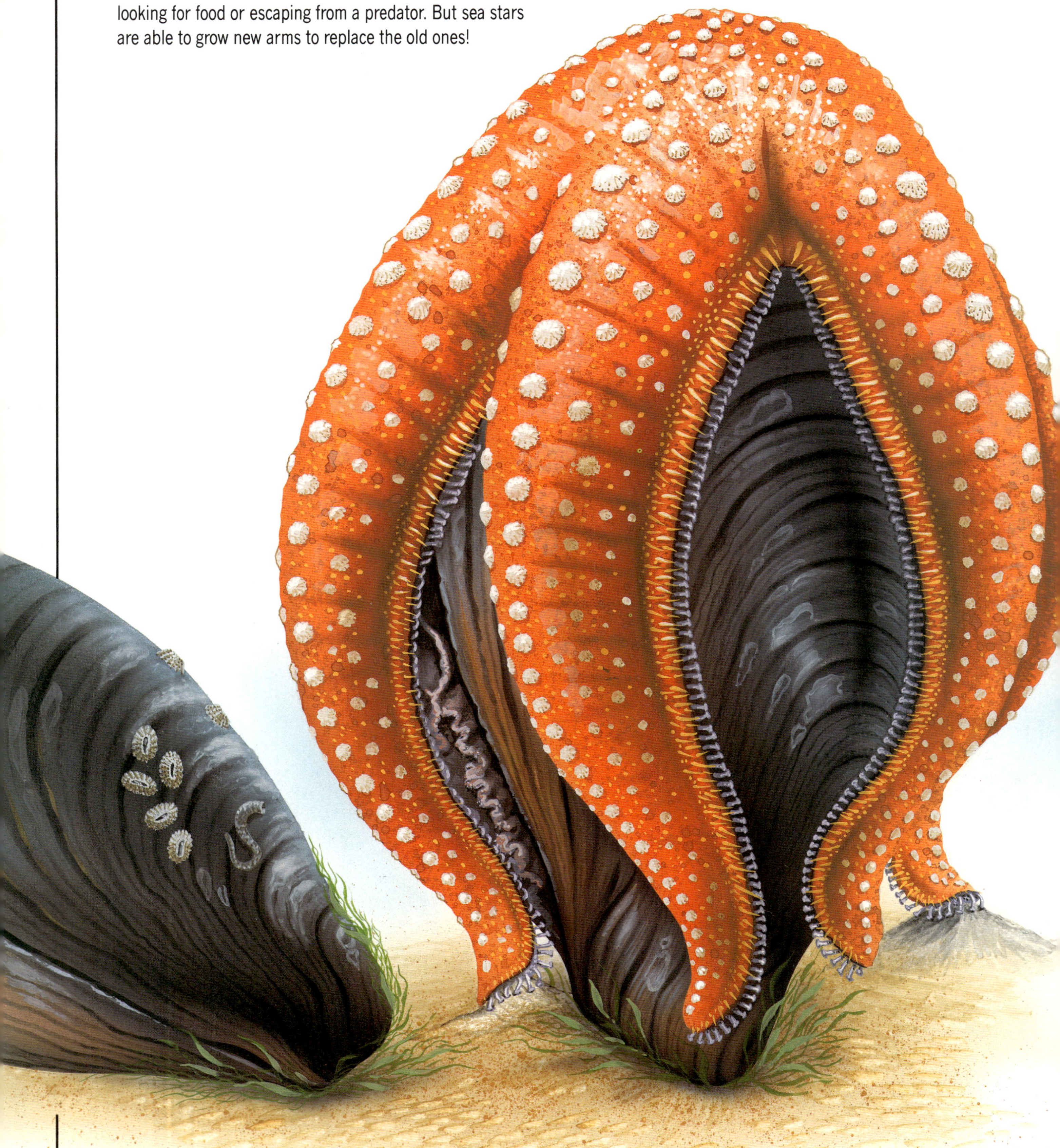

The star-shaped hunter crawls slowly over the rocky reef towards a huge bed of mussels, gripping the surface of the rocks with the suckers on the ends of its tube-feet. The hunter climbs on to a large mussel, carefully positioning its mouth along the line where the two shells of the mussel come together. Gripping tightly, the hunter begins to pull. For several minutes, nothing happens. Then, very slowly, the mussel opens. The hunter forces its stomach bag out of its mouth and through the gap between the shells. Gradually, the stomach bag of the common sea star surround the mussel's soft flesh, and the hunter begins to eat.

Sea stars, also called starfish, are found in all the oceans of the world. Sea stars are not fish. They belong to a group of animals called echinoderms, which includes creatures such as sea urchins and sea cucumbers. There are about 3,600 species of sea star. Some are as small as a human thumbnail, while others are over one metre across. The common sea star has five arms, but other species have more. The common sea star uses the tube-feet which line its arms to move about and grasp its food. Most sea stars eat slow-moving creatures such as worms, mussels, clams and oysters. Others are able to capture swimming crabs and shrimps.

A water canal runs down the centre of each of a sea star's arms. Each canal has several 'branches', and at the end of each branch is a little water-filled sac which sticks out from the creature's body. These sacs are the sea star's 'tube-feet'. By using its muscles, the sea star can squeeze water in and out of its tube-feet, and so propel itself across the sea bed. In most species of sea star, the tips of the tube-feet have suckers, for gripping.

The centre part of a sea star's body is called the disc. A sea star's mouth is on the underside of the disc, in the centre. The mouth opens directly into the stomach.

The Praying Mantis

The predator waits, poised motionless on the branch. Its camouflage is perfect. Only its head tilts slightly as its eyes track the flight of a nearby hoverfly. As the unsuspecting prey flits from flower to flower, searching for nectar, it strays too close to the waiting ambush. Suddenly, the hunter explodes into action. Its spiked forelegs snap like a trap, seizing the hoverfly in a vice-like grip. The hoverfly struggles briefly, pinioned by the hooked limbs, but escape is impossible. The hoverfly is slowly drawn towards the powerful jaws of the hungry praying mantis.

The praying mantis belongs to a group of insects known as mantids, which are found in most warm countries. All of them are fierce hunters. Mantids resemble the shape and sometimes the colour of the plants on which they live. Several species are green and shaped like leaves. Others look like the petals of flowers. Some ground-dwelling mantids can even be mistaken for stones. Their camouflage makes mantids hard to spot and so protects them from other predators. It also makes them successful hunters, and experts at surprise attacks.

A mantid's front legs are armed with sharp spines and hooks. Mantids use their front legs to grab and hold on to their prey. They eat insects, small tree frogs and other mantids.

Mantids have many disguises.

This flower mantid from Malaysia looks like the petals of the flower on which it sits.

The praying mantis gets its name from the way it sits in wait, front legs raised in the air as if in prayer. Like most mantids it can stay completely still for great lengths of time.

African eyed mantid

A mantid has two compound eyes, each of which has many tiny lenses and is very sensitive to movement. It also has three simple eyes set in a triangle between the compound eyes. These simple eyes are very sensitive to light.

Stone-mimicking mantid

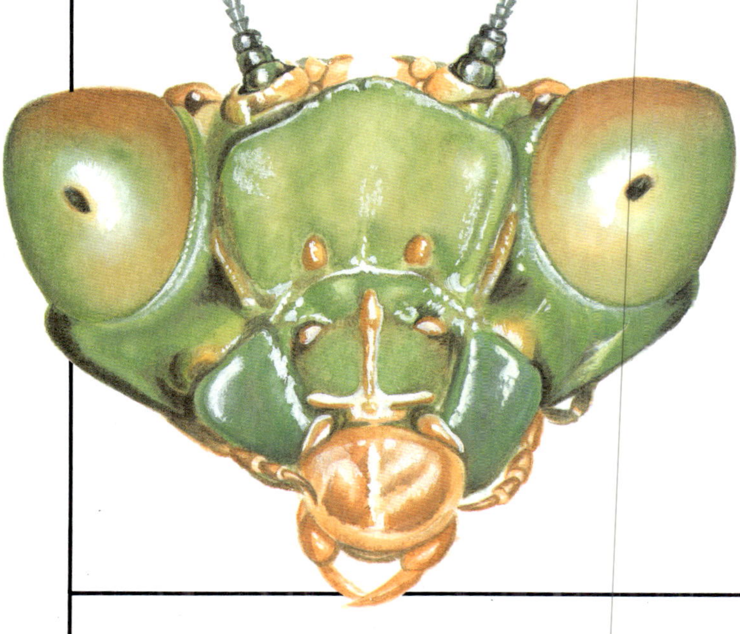

Glossary and Index

abdomen The rear section of an insect's body. The abdomen contains the insect's stomach.

antennae Two long, thin 'feelers' found on the heads of some insects. Antennae are used for smelling and touching.

camouflage Any special shape or colouring which disguises a creature or helps it to hide from its enemies.

grubs The name given to young insects in their first stage of growth.

larvae Another name for grubs. This first stage in a young insect's growth lasts from the time it leaves the egg until it becomes a pupa.

pupae The name given to young insects after they have passed through the grub or larval stage. Pupae develop into adult insects.

venom A poisonous liquid produced by special glands in the bodies of snakes and certain other animals such as spiders. These animals have hollow fangs in their mouths through which they inject their venom into the bodies of their prey.
